My World Atlas

Some important points to help you read the maps!

Borders are marked by white dotted lines.

 Yellow dots symbolize **capitals** whose names are underlined.

 Red dots are used to locate some very **small states** precisely.

 Illustrations highlighted by a little magnifying glass are **explained on the next pages.**

Editorial direction

Galia Lami Dozo – van der Kar

Concept, Illustrations & Layout

Vivi & Gus

Photo credits

©Richard A McMillin/Shutterstock ©Christian Vinces/Shutterstock ©Josef Hanus/Shutterstock ©Iurii Osadchi/Shutterstock ©Richard Seeley/Shutterstock ©Faraways/Shutterstock ©Przemyslaw Skibinski/Shutterstock ©Dan Breckwoldt/Shutterstock ©Pierre-Yves Babelon/Shutterstock ©Graeme Shannon/Shutterstock ©Dario Lo Presti/Shutterstock ©Paolo Bona/Shutterstock ©Petr Jilek/Shutterstock ©ivan bastien/Shutterstock ©Lukiyanova Natalia / frenta/Shutterstock ©AnnaSwiderska/Shutterstock ©waku/Shutterstock ©beboy/Shutterstock ©123Nelson/Shutterstock ©RuthChoi/Shutterstock ©javarman/Shutterstock ©Andres Garcia Martin/Shutterstock ©Migel/Shutterstock ©Anna Kucherova/Shutterstock ©Hung Chung Chih/Shutterstock ©Luciano Morpurgo/Shutterstock ©Tooykrub/Shutterstock ©James van den Broek/Shutterstock ©Debra James/Shutterstock ©THPStock/Shutterstock ©ian woolcock/Shutterstock ©Volodymyr Goinyk/Shutterstock ©Erni/Shutterstock ©Deymos.HR/Shutterstock ©Photoustock/Shutterstock ©Nickola_Che/Shutterstock ©feathercollector/Shutterstock ©diem/Shutterstock ©Elena Mirage/Shutterstock ©takawildcats/Shutterstock ©Matej Hudovernik/Shutterstock ©Yongyut Kumsri/Shutterstock ©Ekaterina Pokrovsky © Zanna Holstova/Shutterstock ©Ondrej Deml/Shutterstock ©Stanislav Fosenbauer/Shutterstock ©Andrey Starostin/Shutterstock

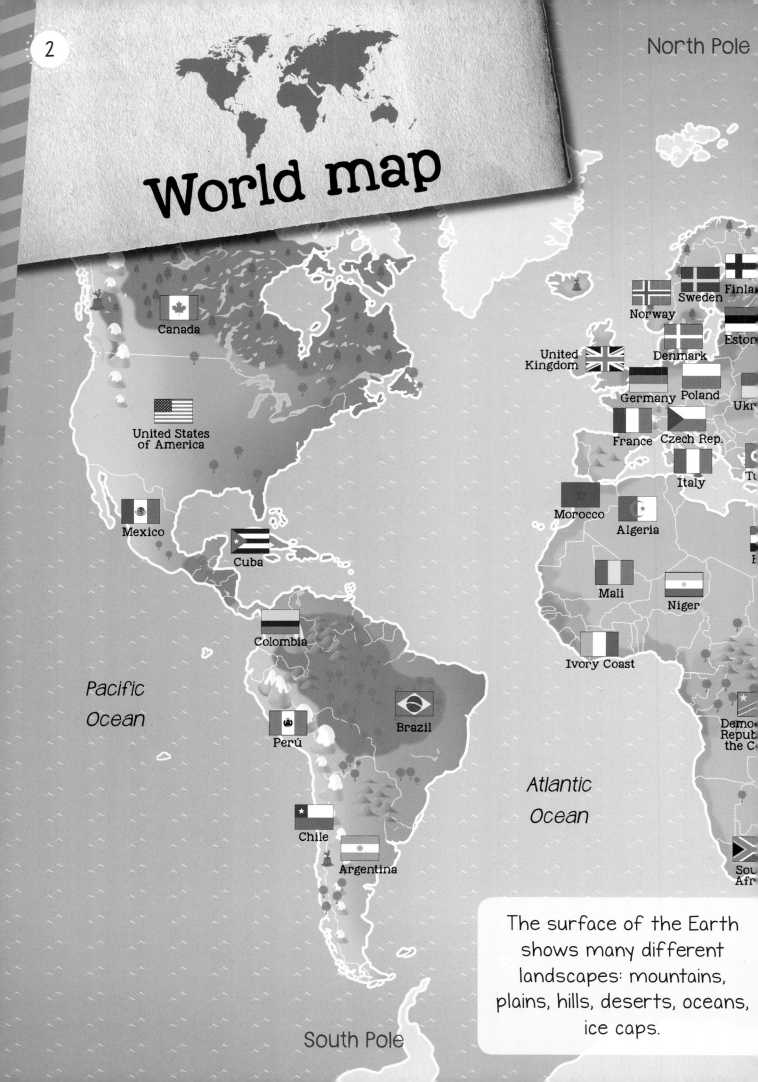

World map

Canada

United States of America

Mexico

Cuba

Colombia

Perú

Brazil

Chile

Argentina

Pacific Ocean

Atlantic Ocean

South Pole

Norway

Sweden

Finla

United Kingdom

Denmark

Eston

Germany

Poland

Ukr

France

Czech Rep.

Italy

Tu

Morocco

Algeria

Mali

Niger

Ivory Coast

Demo Repub the C

Sou Afr

The surface of the Earth shows many different landscapes: mountains, plains, hills, deserts, oceans, ice caps.

193
countries

7
billion
people

6909
languages

Russia

Find the correct flags and stick them on your poster.

China

Japan

South Korea

Pacific Ocean

el

Iran

Saudi Arabia

UAE

India

Thailand

Philippines

iopia

Uganda

Singapore

Solomon Islands

Kenya

Indonesia

Papua New Guinea

Indian Ocean

Australia

Animals and plants adapt to the environment they live in. For example, while the Polar Bear can live on ice in extremely freezing conditions, the brown bear cannot.

New Zealand

The Americas

35 countries

953 million people

1,000 languages

Atlantic Ocean

Maple syrup

Statue of Liberty

New York

OTTAWA

WASHINGTON

The White House

Hamburger & french fries

Hudson Bay

Polar Bear

Mount Rushmore

CANADA

UNITED STATES OF AMERICA

Cowboy

Arctic tern

Moose

Totem

Hollywood

Geyser

Alaska
(United States of America)

Surfing

Find the stickers and stick them where they belong.

MEXICO
CITY OF MEXICO

BELIZE
BELMOPAN

GUATEMALA
GUATEMALA CITY

EL SALVADOR
SAN SALVADOR

HONDURAS
TEGUCIGALPA

NICARAGUA
MANAGUA

COSTA RICA
SAN JOSÉ

PANAMA
PANAMA CITY

CUBA

REPUBLIC
SANTO DOMINGO

JAMAICA
KINGSTON

GUYANA
GEORGETOWN

SURINAME

FRENCH GUIANA

VENEZUELA
BOGOTÁ
CARACAS

COLOMBIA
QUITO

ECUADOR

PERU
LIMA

BRAZIL
Jaguar

BOLIVIA
LA PAZ

PARAGUAY
ASUNCIÓN
BRASILIA

URUGUAY
MONTEVIDEO
BUENOS AIRES

CHILE
SANTIAGO

ARGENTINA

Ara

Toucan

Machu
Picchu

Amazon
rainforest

Rio carnival

Tango

Condor

Penguins

South Pole

Easter
Island

Blue whale

*Pacific
Ocean*

Color the flags

Canada

United States
of America

Argentina

Chile

Colombia

Brazil

Mexico

Cuba

Peru

The Mayas, Incas and Aztecs were brilliant and developed civilisations that lived in the Americas before Christopher Columbus's arrival.

The Americas

The Americas are the second largest continent after Asia. Because of its large size and diverse geographic features, it is divided into North America, Central America, the Caribbean and South America.

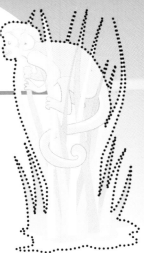

Monkey, Amazonia

Look for the stickers and stick them where they belong.

Over 400 people carved the faces of 4 important American presidents (G. Washington, T. Jefferson, T. Roosevelt and A. Lincoln) to commemorate the first 150 years of the United States of America.

The Native Indians of North America built tall wooden columns called "**totems**". They were carved and shaped like animals and represented the natural and spiritual forces of their tribes.

The **Amazon rainforest** is the world's largest rain forest. More than half of its territory belongs to Brazil. It is named after the Amazon River that runs through it.

Totems

Mount Rushmore

Amazonian rainforest

Moose in Alaska

Ice Hockey in USA and Canada

Magellan Penguins in Patagonia, Argentina

A Moai is a giant one-piece carved stone statue found only on **Easter Island** located 2175 miles off the Chilean coast. The Moai statues are the main attraction on Easter Island, whose inhabitants live from tourism, fishing and agriculture.

Machu Picchu (Peru) is an ancient Inca city, about 550 years old, and is 7,970 feet high, located in the Andes. It was one of the homes of Pachacutec, a famous Inca Emperor. Machu Picchu is considered as a masterpiece of architecture and engineering.

Tango is a musical genre and a sensual dance, characteristic of Argentina. It takes 2 to Tango! Don't get mixed up with Salsa, a more dynamic dance originated in Cuba.

Machu Picchu
Easter Island
Tango

Africa

ALGIERS

TUN

RABAT

MOROCCO

Camels

ALGERIA

Tuareg People

WEST
SAHARA

Giant Acacia

MAURITANIA
NOUAKCHOTT

NIGE

MALI
NIAMEY

BAMAKO

SENEGAL
DAKAR

GAMBIA
BANJUL

**BURKINA
FASO**
OUAGADOUGOU

NIGERI
ABUJA

**GUINEA
BISSAU**
BISSAU

**IVORY
COAST**
YAMOUSSOUKRO

GUINEA
CONAKRY

SIERRA LEONE
FREETOWN

LIBERIA
MONROVIA

CAMEROON

PRÍNCIPE

SÃO TOMÉ
SAO-TOME

GHANA
ACCRA

TOGO
LOME

BENIN
PORTO-NOVO

**EQUATORIAL
GUINEA**
MALABO

GABON
LIBREVILLE

CAP-VERDE

PRAIA

Color the flags

South Africa

Uganda

Kenya

Ethiopia

Mali

Ivory Coast

Algeria

Morocco

Niger

Egypt

Democratic Rep. of The Congo

Atlantic

Ocean

Humpback whale

Find the stickers and
stick them where they
belong.

TUNISIA

POLI

LIBYA

54 countries

1,2 billion people

2,000 languages

CAIRO

Pyramids

The Nile

EGYPT

N
W E
S

CHAD

gmy
eople

N'DJAMENA

Dinka People

SUDAN

KHARTOUM

Dallol, volcanic site in Danakil desert.

ERITREA
ASMARA

DJIBOUTI
DJIBOUTI CITY

ETHIOPIA

ADDIS ABEBA

SOMALIA
MOGADISHU

CENTRAL AFRICAN REPUBLIC

BANGUI

UNDÉ

SOUTH SUDAN

JUBA

UGANDA
KAMPALA

Animals of the Savannah

CONGO

DEMOCRATIC REPUBLIC OF THE CONGO

African rhythms

AZZAVILLE

KINSHASA

RWANDA
KIGALI
BURUNDI
BUJUMBURA

KENYA
NAIROBI

DODOMA

SEYCHELLES
VICTORIA

Kilimanjaro

ANDA

TANZANIA

Zebra

Safari

COMORES
MORONI

ANGOLA

ZAMBIA
LUSAKA

MALAWI
LILONGWE

Victoria Falls

HARARE

ANTANANARIVO

NAMIBIA

ZIMBABWE

MOZAMBIQUE

Lemur

WINDHOEK

BOTSWANA
GABORONE

PRETORIA

MAPUTO

MADAGASCAR

PORT-LOUIS

MAURITIUS

SWAZILAND
LOBAMBA

SOUTH AFRICA

Zulu People

LESOTHO
MASERU

Indian Ocean

There are countless varieties of musical instruments in Africa! Have you tried any of them?

Africa

Africa is the cradle of civilisation! Indeed, the first human being came from there. Africa is a continent with a great diversity of ethnic and cultural populations

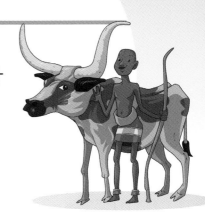

Dinka People

Mbira

The **Egyptian pyramids** are gigantic stone buildings which served as tombs for the pharaohs. There are more than 80 pyramids in Egypt! The largest and most famous ones can be found in Giza.

Egypt pyramids

Blues, jazz, reggae, country, Cuban and Latin music are all variations of African music. The **African rhythms** have influenced all the music in the world, especially in Europe and America.

African rhythms

Kilimanjaro is a big mountain in Tanzania. It is formed by 3 extinct volcanoes: Shira, Mawenzi and Kibo, which is the highest point in Africa. The Kilimanjaro is also known for its famous summit permanently covered by a snow cap!

Kilimanjaro

Tombouctou is a town in Mali. In the Middle Ages, it was a very important commercial centre.

Mother Lemur carrying her baby in Madagascar.

Look for the stickers and stick them where they belong.

Rugby players of South Africa

David Livingstone, the famous Scottish explorer, named these waterfalls after Queen Victoria of the United Kingdom. However, they are known locally as Mosi–oa–Tunya meaning "the smoke that thunders". They are located on the border between Zambia and Zimbabwe.

A **Savannah** is a large piece of land where only herbs, shrubs and very few trees grow. The biggest and most famous savannah regions in the world are in Africa. It is home to lions, zebras, antelope and many other animals.

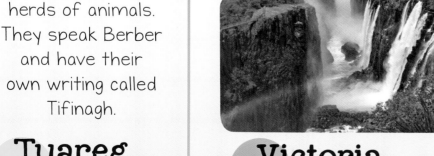

The **Tuaregs** are nomadic populations from the Sahara Desert. They live as extended family units with large herds of animals. They speak Berber and have their own writing called Tifinagh.

Tuareg people

Victoria Falls

African Savannah

Europe

Salmons

Norwegian Sea

Lobster

SWEDEN

NORWAY
OSLO

STOCKHOLM

ICELAND
REYKJAVIK

North Sea

*Balt
Sea*

Giant's Causeway

Sailboat

DENMARK

COPENHAGEN

DUBLIN

IRELAND

UNITED KINGDOM

AMSTERDAM

BERLIN

POLAN

LONDON

THE NETHERLANDS

Berlin wall

Atlantic Ocean

Stonehenge

BELGIUM

BRUSSELS

GERMANY

PRAGUE

CZECH REP.

SLOVA

PARIS

LUXEMBURG
LUXEMBURG

VIENNA

BRATI

BUDAPE

Eiffel Tower

LIECHTENSTEIN

SWITZERLAND
BERN

AUSTRIA

HUNG.

SLOVENIA

ZAGRE

French cheese

LJUBLJANA

CROATI

FRANCE

**BOSNI
HERZEGOV**

SPAIN

MONACO

ST MARIN

SARAJE

PORTUGAL

ANDORRA

Pisa
Corsica

MONTENE
PODG

ROME

LISBON

MADRID

Flamenco

VATICAN CITY

ITALY

Tyrrhenian Sea

Sardinia

Mediterranean Sea

Io
S

Etna in Sicily

Stickers for the poster

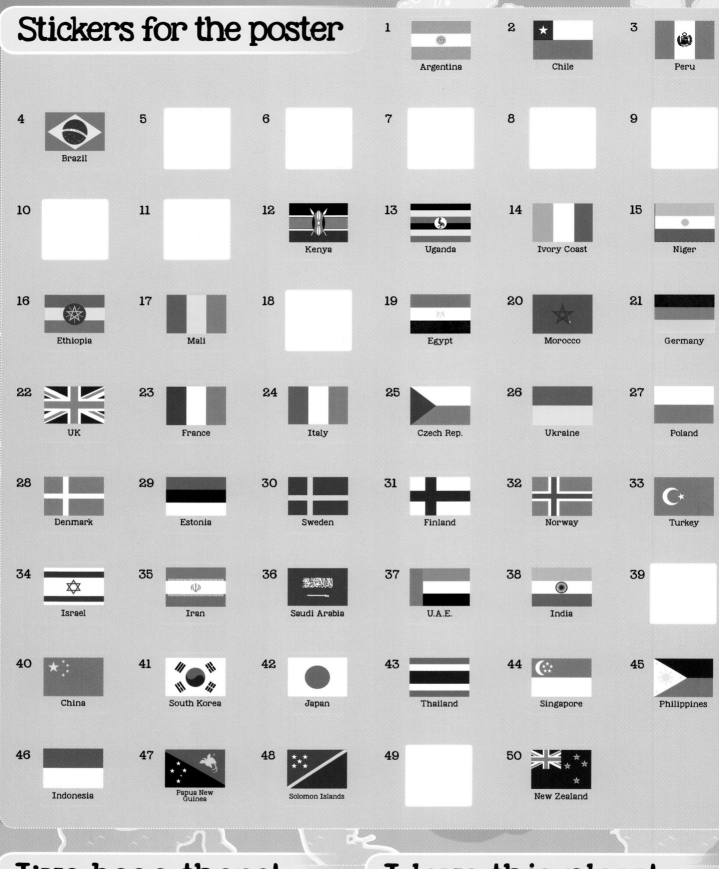

1	Argentina
2	Chile
3	Peru
4	Brazil
5	
6	
7	
8	
9	
10	
11	
12	Kenya
13	Uganda
14	Ivory Coast
15	Niger
16	Ethiopia
17	Mali
18	
19	Egypt
20	Morocco
21	Germany
22	UK
23	France
24	Italy
25	Czech Rep.
26	Ukraine
27	Poland
28	Denmark
29	Estonia
30	Sweden
31	Finland
32	Norway
33	Turkey
34	Israel
35	Iran
36	Saudi Arabia
37	U.A.E.
38	India
39	
40	China
41	South Korea
42	Japan
43	Thailand
44	Singapore
45	Philippines
46	Indonesia
47	Papua New Guinea
48	Solomon Islands
49	
50	New Zealand

I've been there!

I love this place!

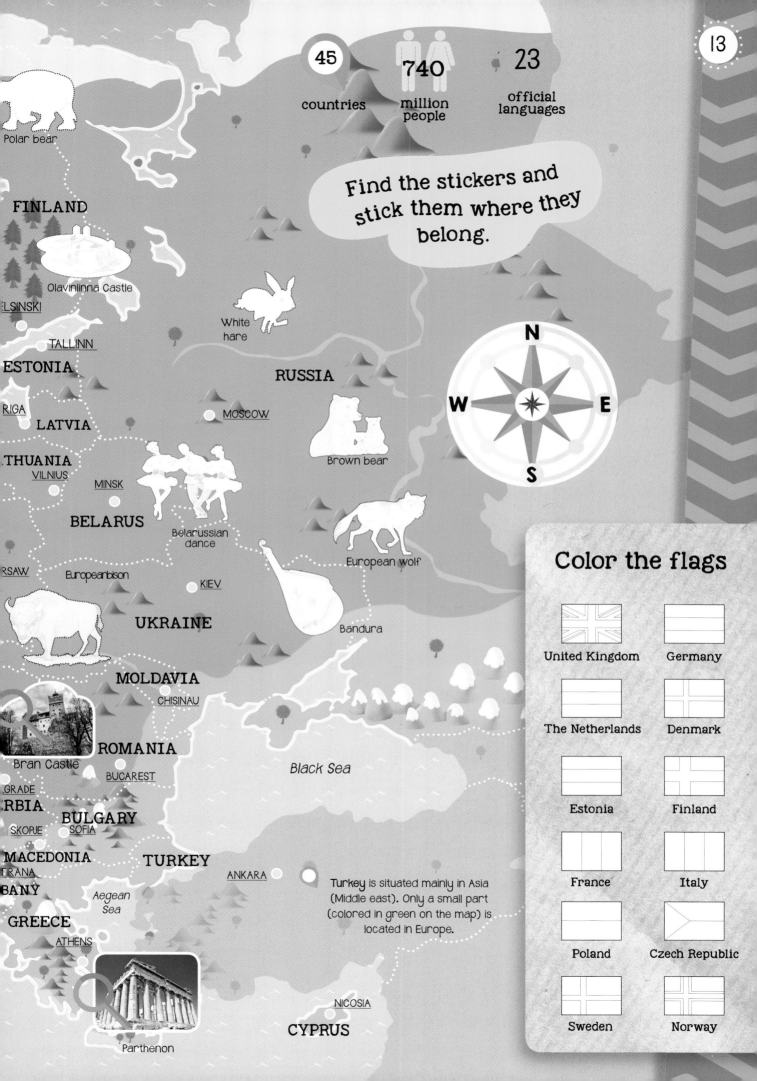

Europe

The European civilisation comes from many different cultures and has a rich historical past. Its name comes from Greek mythology: it was the name of a Phoenician princess. Most of the European countries are part of the European Union (an economic and political union).

European Bison

In the south of England, there is a place called "**Stonehenge**", which is one of the most important prehistoric monuments in the world. Some say it was a temple, others say that it was a sort of prehistoric calendar. There are many theories, but none seems to answer the mystery.

Flamenco is originally from Andalusia, Spain. This famous dance and music is the result of a cultural mix of Gypsy and Arabic influence. It is well known for its rhythmed arm movements and guitar riffs.

The **Tower of Pisa** in Italy is the bell tower of the Cathedral of Pisa. The tower began to lean as soon as it was built. To prevent its collapse, engineers have recently stabilized the tower, which should stop it from leaning further and falling over.

Stonehenge

Flamenco

Tower of Pisa

The famous chain bridge in Budapest, Hungary

Krakow market square at sunset (Poland)

The Eiffel Tower, Paris, France

Find the stickers and stick them where they belong.

Bran Castle is a medieval fortress in Romania. Bram Stoker, author of the book on Count Dracula, was inspired by this castle and used it as Dracula's home.

Etna is one of the most active volcanoes in the world located on the island of Sicily, in Italy. In 2014, it erupted 3 times and has since formed a new crater.

The Parthenon is one of the most important monuments of ancient Greece. It was built in white marble and contained a 40 foot tall statue of Athena Parthenos made of gold and ivory!

Bran Castle

Etna

Parthenon

Asia

49 countries

4,4 billion people

2,000 languages

RUSSIA

Matryoshka doll

European wolf

MOSCOW

Cossack Dance

ASTANA

Yurt

KAZAKHSTAN

GEORGIA

AZERBAIJAN

ARMENIA

TBILISI

Caspian Sea

BAKU

UZBEKISTAN

BISHKEK

KYRGYZSTAN

TASHKENT

Turkey is situated mainly in Asia (Middle east). The part colored in green on the map is located in Asia.

ANKARA

YEREVAN

TURKMENISTAN

TAJIKISTAN

ASHGABAT

DUSHANBE

TURKEY

SYRIA

DAMASCUS

TEHRAN

IRAN

ISLAMABAD

Chinese dragon

LEBANON

BEIRUT

BAGHDAD

KABUL

AFGHANISTAN

NEW DELHI

NEP.
KATHM.

IRAQ

AMMAN

Yazd

PAKISTAN

ISRAEL

JERUSALEM

KUWAIT

KUWAIT CITY

BAHREIN

MANAMA

SAUDI ARABIA

RIYADH

QATAR

DOHA

ABU DHABI

MUSCAT

Taj.

JORDAN

Arabian Sea

INDIA

Camel

U.A.E.

OMAN

YEMEN

SANA'A

The cow: "sacred animal". India

Indian people

SRI JAYAWARDENEPU - KO

S.
LAN

MALDIVES

MALE

Indian Ocean

Color the flags

Indonesia

Iran

Philippines

India

Japan

Russia

Saudi Arabia

China

Thailand

Turkey

U.A.E.

Singapore

South Korea

Israel

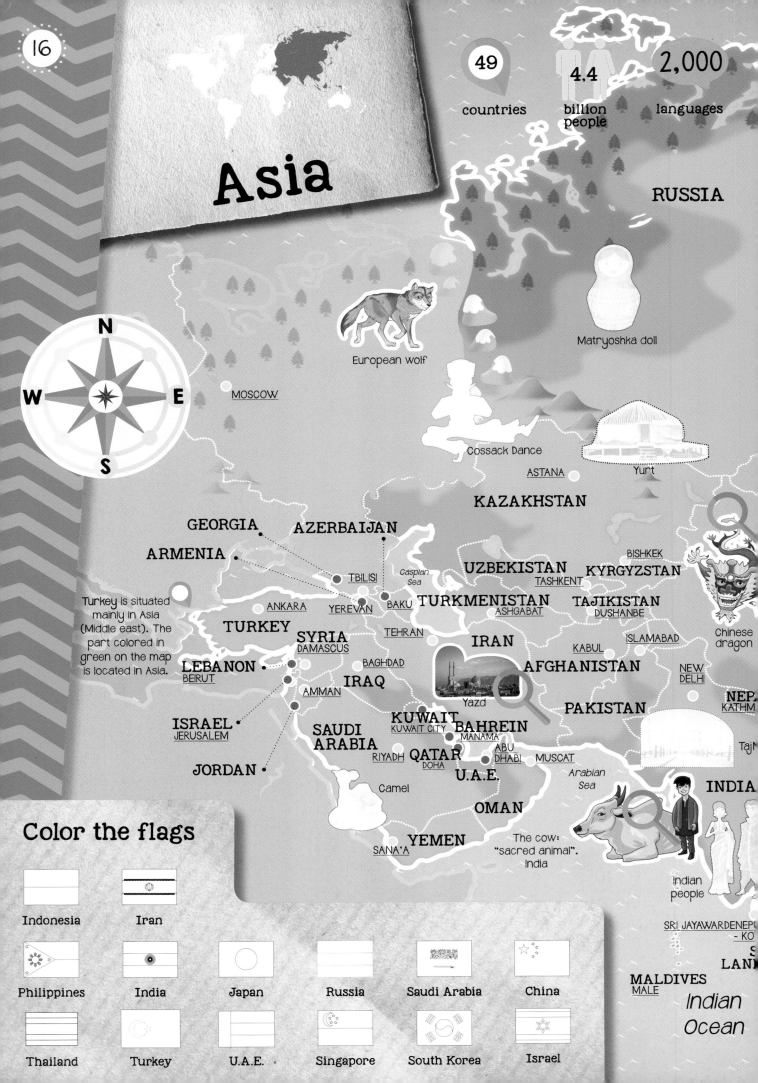

Chukchi people

Russia is the largest country in the world. A small part of Russia is located in Europe, but the majority of it is located in Asia.

Siberian stag

Pelmeni

Trans-Siberian Railway

Amur leopard

Fishing boat

Pacific Ocean

ULAANBAATAR

MONGOLIA

NORTH KOREA
PYONGYANG

Sea of Japan

JAPAN
TOKYO

Sushi

BEIJING

HINA

Great wall

SEOUL

SOUTH KOREA

The Daibutsu-den temple in Nara, Japan

anda bear

BHUTAN
THIMPHU

chinese palace

HAKA

IGLADESH

MYANMAR
NAYPYIDAW

VIETNAM
HANOI

LAOS
VIENTIANE

Tian Tian Buddha (Hong-Kong)

TAIPEI

TAIWAN

THAILAND
BANGKOK

CAMBODIA
PHNOM PENH

MANILA

PHILIPPINES

Find the stickers and stick them where they belong.

BRUNEI
BANDAR SERI BEGAWAN

KUALA LUMPUR

MALAYSIA

Petronas Twin Towers.
Kuala Lumpur

INDONESIA

SINGAPORE
SINGAPORE

Komodo dragon

JAKARTA

DILI

TIMOR-LESTE

Asia is the most populated continent in the world. Its population is concentrated mostly in China, India and Indonesia!

Asia

Asia is the largest continent on Earth and continues to experience rapid economic growth. It is also in Asia that we can find both the highest peak in the world – Mount Everest, and the deepest valley – the Dead Sea, which is located between Israel and Jordan.

Tiger in India

In Antiquity, this country was called the Persian Empire. Nowadays, the official language is Persian. **Iran**, along with Iraq, used to be the cradle of one of the oldest civilizations in the world. It is said that the Garden of Eden was in the actual city of Tabriz.

The **Cow** is a sacred animal in India. You aren't allowed to eat them. They do not have a master and wander freely, even in the city streets. They are often the cause of traffic jams!

Indonesia is famous for the many unique animals that live there. The Tarsier or **Komodo Dragon** to name two. It is important to protect these animals because many of them are endangered species.

Iran

Sacred cow

Komodo dragon

Dome of the Rock, Jerusalem, Israel

Great Wall of China

Taj Mahal, India

Find the stickers and stick them where they belong.

Sushi is generally prepared and served in small portions and different shapes. It is often prepared with raw fish, seafood, rice, vegetables and even with eggs. This typical Japanese dish was originally an ancient Chinese meal! Have you tried it?

Sushi

The **Chukchi's** live in Siberia. They work in mining, fishing and reindeer herding. Due to the low temperatures in the region, the Chukchi's are experts in the manufacturing of warm clothes made from reindeer fur.

Chukchi people

The Chinese New Year is the most awaited festival in China. It is a very lively and colorful celebration where **Chinese dragons,** carried by many dancers, chase off evil spirits.

Chinese dragon

Oceania

Find the stickers and stick them where they belong.

N
W E
S

Great White Shark

Indian
Ocean

Aborigine

Kangaroo

Seahorse

Blue whale

Color the flags

Australia

Solomon Islands

New Zealand

Papua
New Guinea

Giant squid

14 countries

38 million people

1,000 languages

Echidna

Masc Dagak

PAPUA NEW GUINEA

PORT MORESBY

Papuan people

SOLOMON ISLANDS

HONIARA

Crocodile

Frill necked lizard

AUSTRALIA

Great Barrier Reef

Uluru or Ayers rock

Boomerang

Emu

Koala

SYDNEY

CANBERRA

Sydney's Opera House

Box jellyfish

WELLINGTON

Tasmanian devil

Surfing

Pacific Ocean

NEW ZEALAND

Kiwi

Antarctica ↓

Platypus

Oceania

Oceania is the smallest continent and least populated. It is composed of many islands in all shapes and sizes. Australia is the biggest island in Oceania and also in the world! Most of the centre of Australia is made up of very hot deserts and savannahs! The population lives mostly in cities along the coast line. Some of the most amazing animals live in Australia, such as the kangaroo, the koala, the Tasmanian devil and the duckbilled platypus.

Sydney's Opera House is one of the most famous landmarks in Australia. It has 5 theatres, 5 studios, 2 concert halls, 4 restaurants and a souvenir shop. It is also used for weddings, parties and conferences.

The **koala** is not a bear, it's a marsupial. It lives in eucalyptus trees whose leaves it likes to eat. Most of all, the koala loves to sleep, sometimes up to 18 hours a day!

Ayers rock, also known by its Aboriginal name 'Uluru', is an isolated mountain located in central Australia. It is all that is left of an original mountain range which has slowly eroded away.

Sydney's Opera House

Koala

Ayers rock

Cradle Mountain and Dove Lake in Tasmania

Find the stickers and stick them where they belong.

The venom of this Australian tarantula can kill a person in less than 2 hours!

Australian kangaroo with a joey in its pouch

The **box jellyfish** is one of the most venomous animals in the world. It is almost transparent and got its name from the cube–like shape of its head. It has a total of 24 eyes and its tentacles can be up to 10 feet long.

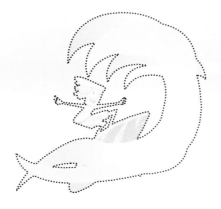

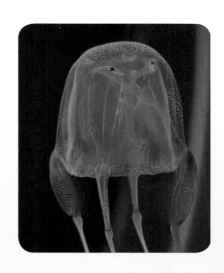

The **Great Barrier Reef** is the largest coral reef in the world. It's a great spot for scuba divers, and is so large that it can be seen from space.

Australia is one of the greatest places in the world for **Surfing**, but beware as Australia's waters are filled with many sharks. The Gold Coast has the best waves in the world. Thousands of tourists from around the world go there to ride them.

Great Barrier Reef

Surfing

Box Jellyfish

Arctic & Antarctic

There are two very cold zones on earth: one is located at the northern most part of our planet and the other at the southern most part.

North Pole

Equator

South Pole

The **Arctic** (North Pole) is in fact an ocean partly covered by a thick ice cap. In summer, enormous blocks of ice breaks off and form icebergs. The Arctic is surrounded by the icy landscapes of Canada, Russia and Sweden.

Arctic hare, lemming, muskox, caribou, snowy owl, arctic fox, wolf and polar bear are some of the animals that live there.

Antarctica is the 6th continent on Earth located in the South Pole. It is mostly covered by ice and snow and contains about 80% of the fresh water reserve of our planet.

Most of the animals living on this continent are found in the oceans that surround it: giant jellyfish, whales, seals, penguins... as well as thousands of birds!